THIS BOOK BELONGS TO

"You're braver than you believe, and stronger than you seem, and smarter than you think."

—CHRISTOPHER ROBIN.

ANY CHILD USING THIS WORKBOOK SHOULD DO SO WITH THE GUIDANCE OF A PARENT, COUNSELLOR, OR OTHER QUALIFIED MENTAL HEALTH PROFESSIONAL. CHILDREN SHOULD NOT BE EXPECTED TO WORK THROUGH THIS BOOK ON THEIR OWN. ALTHOUGH CONCEPTS HAVE BEEN SIMPLIFIED TO MAXIMIZE THE CHILD'S INDEPENDENT USE OF THIS BOOK, SUPPORT IS STILL REQUIRED TO ENSURE COMPREHENSION AND MAXIMUM BENEFIT

KEEP THIS BOOK IN A SAFE PLACE SO YOU CAN LOOK AT IT WHENEVER YOU WANT. LOOKING THROUGH THIS BOOK WILL HELP YOU REMEMBER YOUR BODY TOOLS, THINKING TOOLS, AND FEELING TOOLS. WHEN YOU LOOK AT THIS BOOK, REMEMBER HOW STRONG AND BRAVE YOU ARE FOR LEARNING TO MANAGE YOUR BIG FEELINGS!

STAY STRONG & POWER ON

NO MATTER WHAT
HAPPENS WHEN YOU ARE
ANXIOUS AND STRESSED,
IT'S
IMPORTANT TO HAVE A
PLAN TO HELP YOURSELF
STAY SAFE, CALM
DOWN AND FEEL BETTER.

A PEEK INSIDE MY MIND

In these clouds, write down all of your thoughts and feelings that are having. They can be happy thoughts, sad thoughts, worried thoughts, excited thoughts!

THE STORY OF YOU

You can write or draw your story!

In the boxes below, share your story! What important events have happened in your life? What are your strongest memories? What hobbies or passions are important to you?

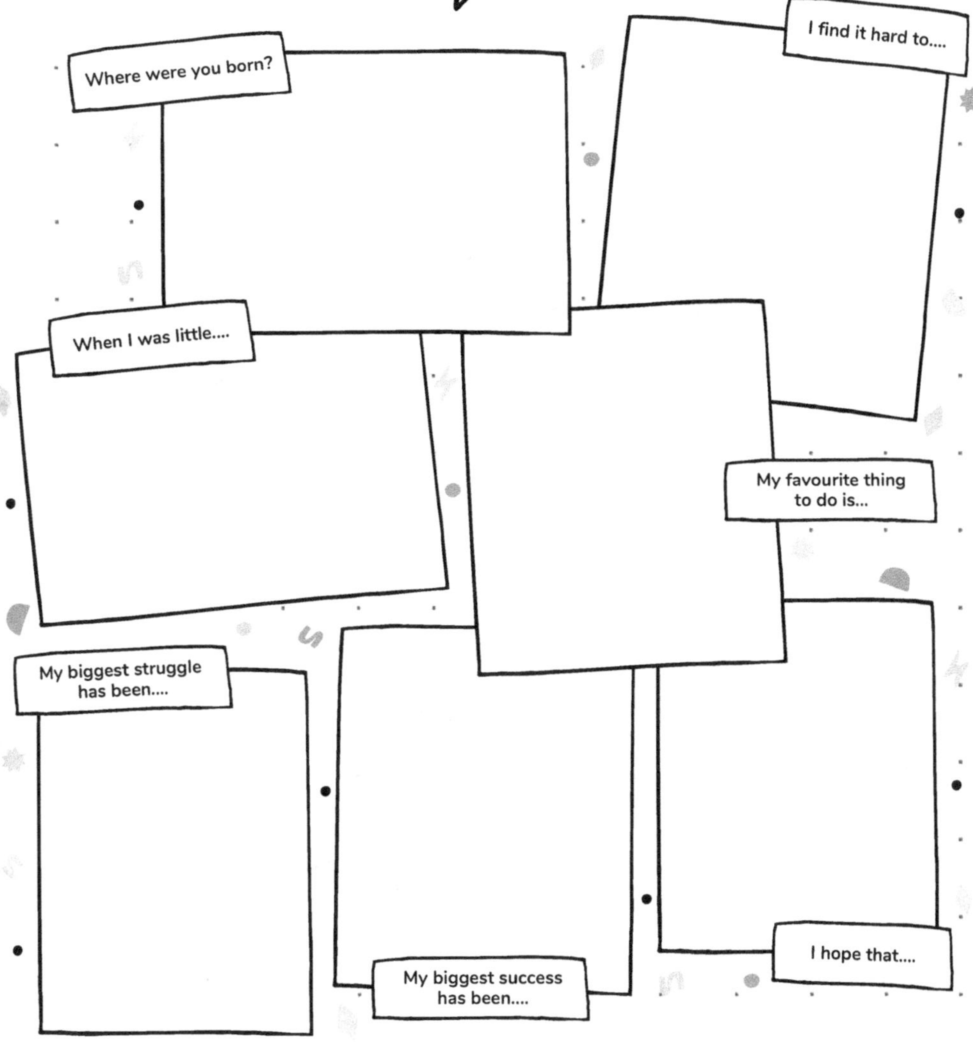

What makes you anxious & Stressed ?

Things You Can Do to deal with anxiety, stress, fear, panic attacks

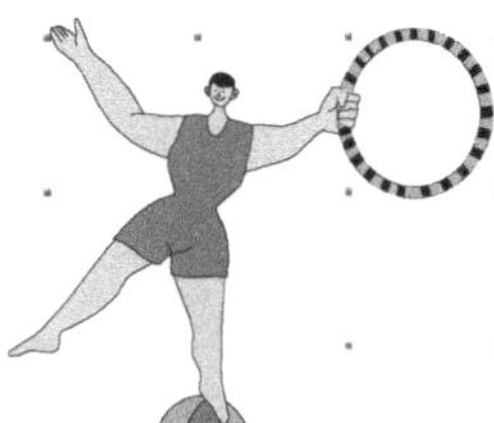

*Focus Your Brain On Another Activity (read a book, play a computer game, do a puzzle, watch television)

*Participate In A Physical Activity Or Sport

*Use Deep Breathing Exercises

*Imagine Yourself In A Special Place

*Think Positively Using Affirmations

*Find Something Funny That Will Make You Laugh

*Write Your Worries In A Journal

What is a Worry?

WRITE OR DRAW ABOUT IT

DRAW YOUR ANGRY FACE

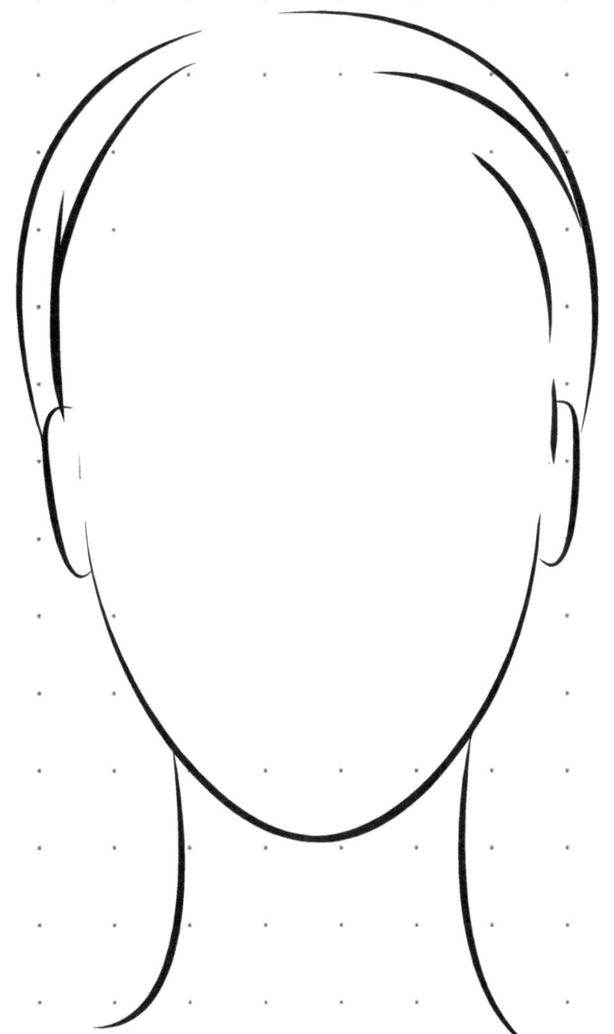

Positive Affirmations

I AM A WINNER	I AM PEACEFUL	I AM PROUD OF WHAT I'VE DONE	I AM BRAVE	I LIKE MY BODY
I MAKE GOOD CHOICES	I AM STRONG	FACE FEARS	I CAN DO IT	I'LL TRY MY BEST AND THAT WILL BE GOOD ENOUGH
I WILL STAY CALM AND RELAXED	I AM SAFE	*i'm free*	I WILL DO A GREAT JOB	BE KIND TO YOURSELF
HONOR YOUR WORD TO OTHERS	REMIND YOURSELF YOU ARE ENOUGH	LOVE YOURSELF MORE THAN OTHERS WILL	DREAM BIG AND MAKE IT HAPPEN	CHALLENGE LIMITING BELIEFS
HELP SOMEONE	STOP WORRYING ABOUT WHAT OTHERS THINK	HEAL YOUR PAST	READ SOMETHING INSPIRATIONAL	RECLAIM INTEGRITY

Your own Positive Affirmations

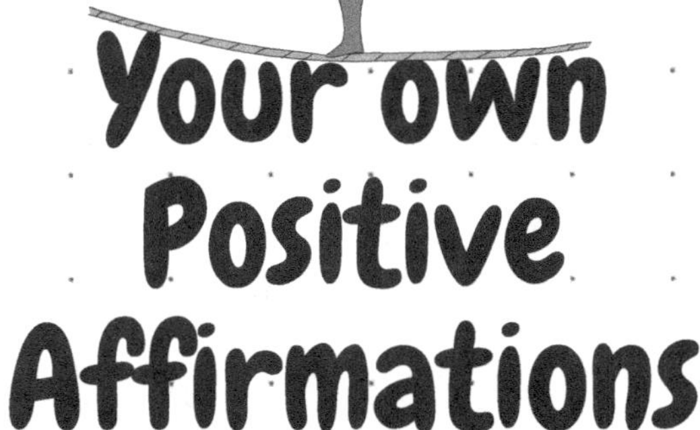

I felt angry when

I felt angry when

Self-care is when you take time to do things that make your mind and body feel calm and happy. By taking care of yourself often, you are better able to cope with stress or other feelings that you may experience.

WHAT HEALTHY FOODS DO YOU LIKE TO EAT?

WHAT FUN ACTIVITIES CAN YOU DO TO KEEP YOUR BODY HEALTHY?

Healthy body challenge

Every time you eat healthy food, give
yourself one star.

Date   Week one

HEALTHY FOOD CHALLENGE

| MONDAY | TUESDAY | FUN ACTIVITIES |

| WEDNESDAY | THURSDAY |

| FRIDAY | SATURDAY |

| SUNDAY | NOTES |

Date   Week Two

HEALTHY FOOD CHALLENGE

MONDAY	TUESDAY	FUN ACTIVITIES
WEDNESDAY	THURSDAY	
FRIDAY	SATURDAY	
SUNDAY	NOTES	

Every time you eat healthy food, give yourself one star.

Date   Week Three

HEALTHY FOOD CHALLENGE

MONDAY

TUESDAY

FUN ACTIVITIES

WEDNESDAY

THURSDAY

FRIDAY

SATURDAY

SUNDAY

NOTES

Every time you eat healthy food, give yourself one star.

Date   Week Four

HEALTHY FOOD CHALLENGE

MONDAY

TUESDAY

FUN ACTIVITIES

WEDNESDAY

THURSDAY

FRIDAY

SATURDAY

SUNDAY

NOTES

MY SPECIAL PLAN IS FOR :

WHEN I FEEL :

I CAN :

MY SPECIAL PLAN IS FOR :

WHEN I FEEL :

I CAN :

MY SPECIAL PLAN IS FOR :

<u>WHEN I FEEL :</u>

I CAN :

MY SPECIAL PLAN IS FOR :

WHEN I FEEL :

I CAN :

MY SPECIAL PLAN IS FOR :

WHEN I FEEL :

I CAN :

MY SPECIAL PLAN IS FOR :

WHEN I FEEL :

I CAN :

MY SPECIAL PLAN IS FOR :

WHEN I FEEL :

I CAN :

MY SPECIAL PLAN IS FOR :

WHEN I FEEL :

I CAN :

MY SPECIAL PLAN IS FOR :

WHEN I FEEL :

I CAN :

MY SPECIAL PLAN IS FOR :

WHEN I FEEL :

I CAN :

WORRY TRACKER

DATE :

MY WORRY	TIME & PLACE	WHAT HAPPENED BEFORE MY WORRY STARTED

HOW MY BODY FELT	STRATEGY I USED TO FEEL BETTER	NOTES

WORRY TRACKER

DATE :

MY WORRY	TIME & PLACE	WHAT HAPPENED BEFORE MY WORRY STARTED

HOW MY BODY FELT	STRATEGY I USED TO FEEL BETTER	NOTES

WORRY TRACKER

DATE :

MY WORRY	TIME & PLACE	WHAT HAPPENED BEFORE MY WORRY STARTED

HOW MY BODY FELT	STRATEGY I USED TO FEEL BETTER	NOTES

WORRY TRACKER

MY WORRY	TIME & PLACE	WHAT HAPPENED BEFORE MY WORRY STARTED
HOW MY BODY FELT	STRATEGY I USED TO FEEL BETTER	NOTES

WORRY TRACKER

DATE :

MY WORRY	TIME & PLACE	WHAT HAPPENED BEFORE MY WORRY STARTED

HOW MY BODY FELT	STRATEGY I USED TO FEEL BETTER	NOTES

WORRY TRACKER

DATE :

MY WORRY	TIME & PLACE	WHAT HAPPENED BEFORE MY WORRY STARTED

HOW MY BODY FELT	STRATEGY I USED TO FEEL BETTER	NOTES

WORRY TRACKER

DATE :

MY WORRY	TIME & PLACE	WHAT HAPPENED BEFORE MY WORRY STARTED

HOW MY BODY FELT	STRATEGY I USED TO FEEL BETTER	NOTES

WORRY TRACKER

DATE :

MY WORRY	TIME & PLACE	WHAT HAPPENED BEFORE MY WORRY STARTED
HOW MY BODY FELT	STRATEGY I USED TO FEEL BETTER	NOTES

WORRY TRACKER

DATE :

| MY WORRY | TIME & PLACE | WHAT HAPPENED BEFORE MY WORRY STARTED |

| HOW MY BODY FELT | STRATEGY I USED TO FEEL BETTER | NOTES |

WORRY TRACKER

DATE :

MY WORRY	TIME & PLACE	WHAT HAPPENED BEFORE MY WORRY STARTED

HOW MY BODY FELT	STRATEGY I USED TO FEEL BETTER	NOTES

WORRY TRACKER

DATE :

MY WORRY	TIME & PLACE	WHAT HAPPENED BEFORE MY WORRY STARTED

HOW MY BODY FELT	STRATEGY I USED TO FEEL BETTER	NOTES

WORRY TRACKER

DATE :

MY WORRY	TIME & PLACE	WHAT HAPPENED BEFORE MY WORRY STARTED

HOW MY BODY FELT	STRATEGY I USED TO FEEL BETTER	NOTES

KoglinArt

WORRY TRACKER

DATE :

MY WORRY	TIME & PLACE	WHAT HAPPENED BEFORE MY WORRY STARTED

HOW MY BODY FELT	STRATEGY I USED TO FEEL BETTER	NOTES

WORRY TRACKER

DATE :

| MY WORRY | TIME & PLACE | WHAT HAPPENED BEFORE MY WORRY STARTED |
| HOW MY BODY FELT | STRATEGY I USED TO FEEL BETTER | NOTES |

WORRY TRACKER

DATE :

MY WORRY	TIME & PLACE	WHAT HAPPENED BEFORE MY WORRY STARTED

HOW MY BODY FELT	STRATEGY I USED TO FEEL BETTER	NOTES

WORRY TRACKER

DATE :

MY WORRY	TIME & PLACE	WHAT HAPPENED BEFORE MY WORRY STARTED
HOW MY BODY FELT	STRATEGY I USED TO FEEL BETTER	NOTES

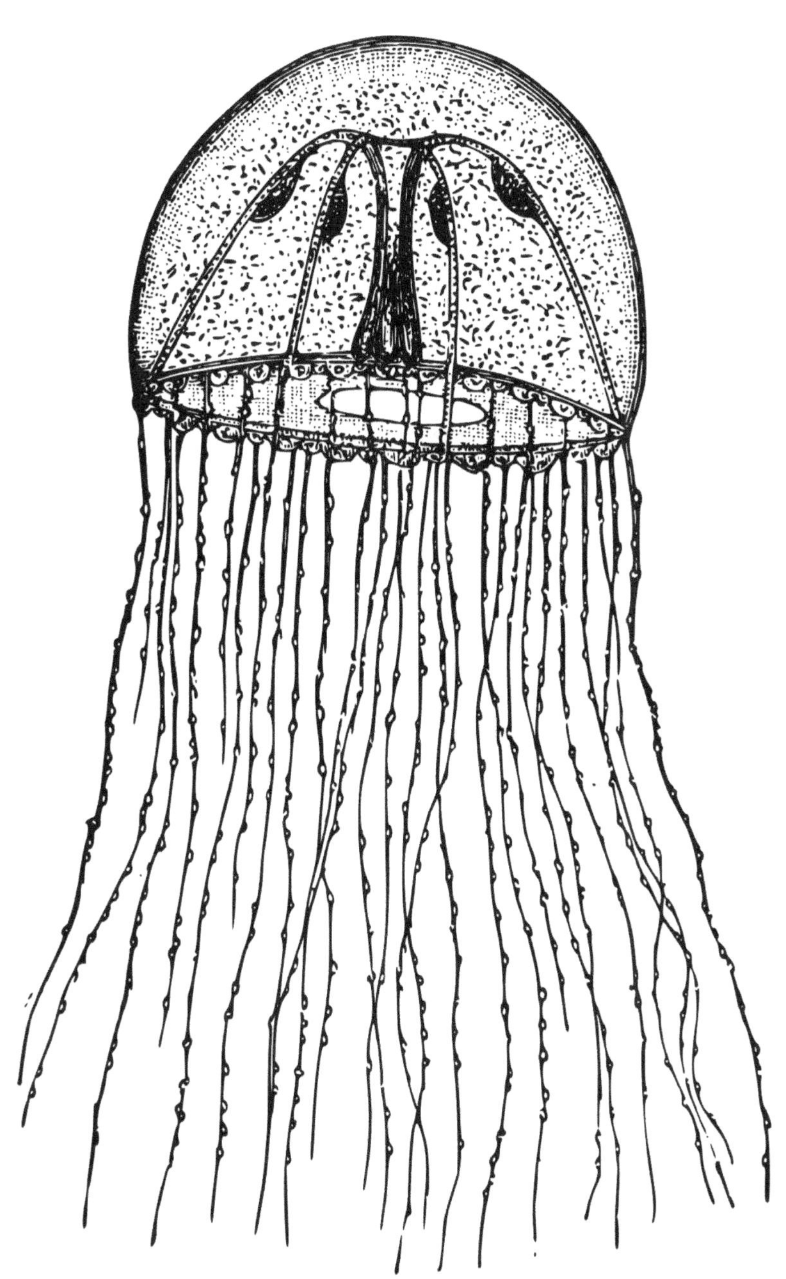

WORRY TRACKER

DATE :

MY WORRY	TIME & PLACE	WHAT HAPPENED BEFORE MY WORRY STARTED

HOW MY BODY FELT	STRATEGY I USED TO FEEL BETTER	NOTES

COLOR THAT SHAPE

Let's decorate this pizza! Follow the color guide and color the shapes. When done, count how many of each shape are in the pizza and write them in the boxes below.

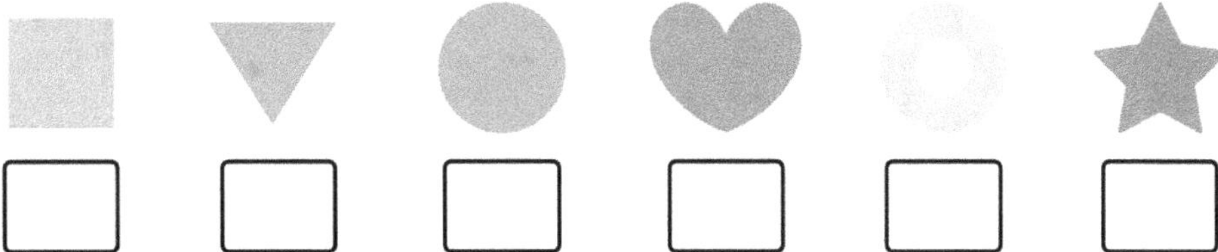

WORRY TRACKER

DATE :

MY WORRY	TIME & PLACE	WHAT HAPPENED BEFORE MY WORRY STARTED

HOW MY BODY FELT	STRATEGY I USED TO FEEL BETTER	NOTES

WORRY TRACKER

DATE :

MY WORRY	TIME & PLACE	WHAT HAPPENED BEFORE MY WORRY STARTED

HOW MY BODY FELT	STRATEGY I USED TO FEEL BETTER	NOTES

NAME THAT POLYGON!

Can you name these polygons according to the number of their sides?

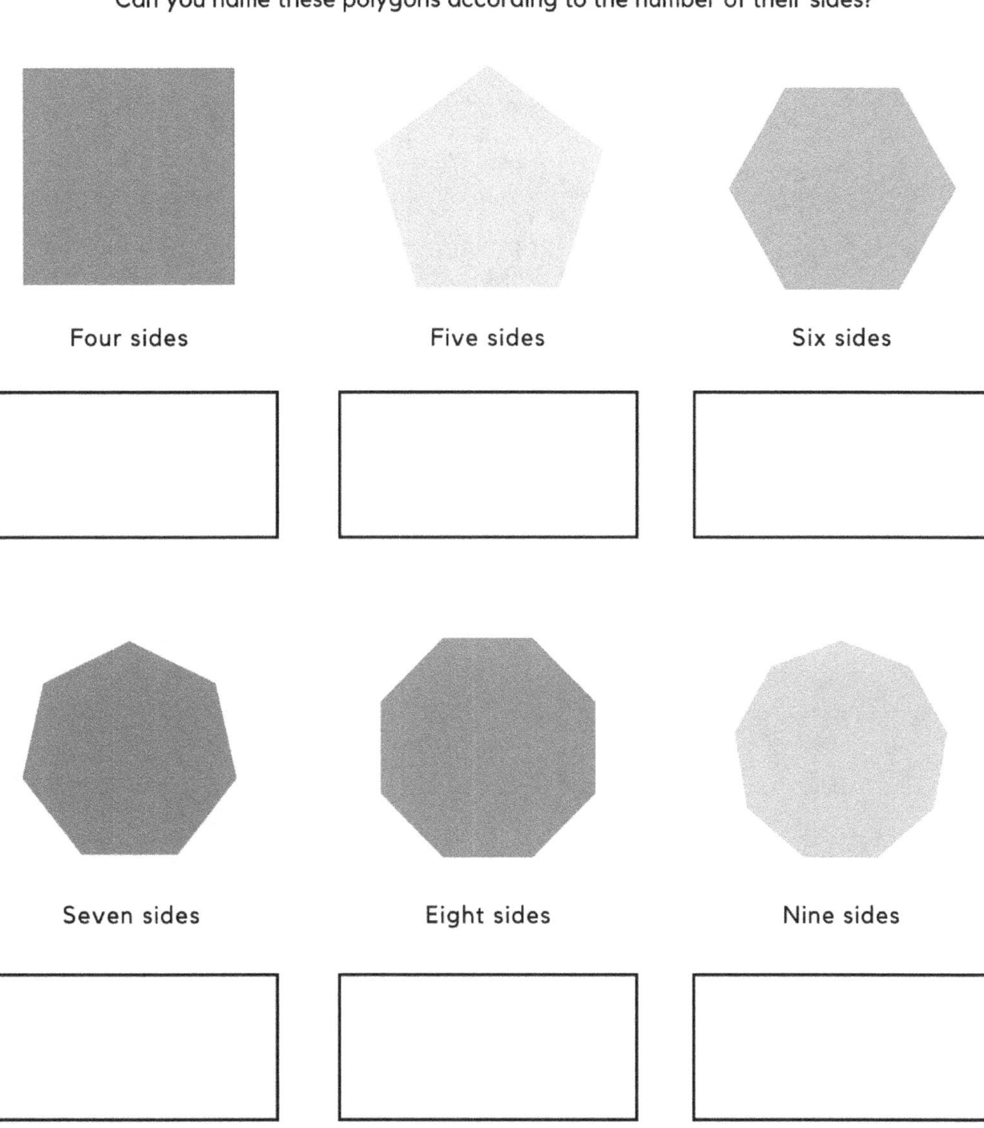

WORRY TRACKER

DATE :

MY WORRY	TIME & PLACE	WHAT HAPPENED BEFORE MY WORRY STARTED
HOW MY BODY FELT	STRATEGY I USED TO FEEL BETTER	NOTES

WORRY TRACKER

DATE :

| MY WORRY | TIME & PLACE | WHAT HAPPENED BEFORE MY WORRY STARTED |

| HOW MY BODY FELT | STRATEGY I USED TO FEEL BETTER | NOTES |

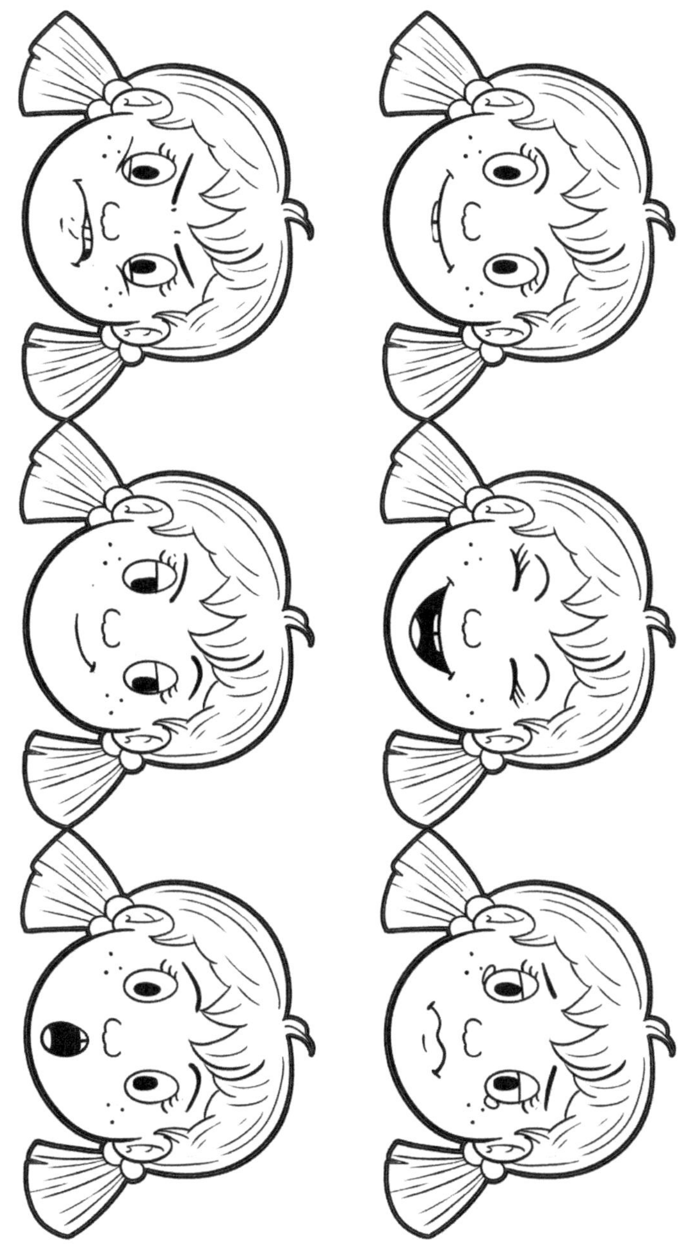

WORRY TRACKER

DATE :

MY WORRY	TIME & PLACE	WHAT HAPPENED BEFORE MY WORRY STARTED
HOW MY BODY FELT	STRATEGY I USED TO FEEL BETTER	NOTES

WORRY TRACKER

DATE :

MY WORRY	TIME & PLACE	WHAT HAPPENED BEFORE MY WORRY STARTED
HOW MY BODY FELT	STRATEGY I USED TO FEEL BETTER	NOTES

WORRY TRACKER

DATE :

MY WORRY	TIME & PLACE	WHAT HAPPENED BEFORE MY WORRY STARTED

HOW MY BODY FELT	STRATEGY I USED TO FEEL BETTER	NOTES

WORRY TRACKER

DATE :

MY WORRY	TIME & PLACE	WHAT HAPPENED BEFORE MY WORRY STARTED

HOW MY BODY FELT	STRATEGY I USED TO FEEL BETTER	NOTES

WORRY TRACKER

DATE :

MY WORRY	TIME & PLACE	WHAT HAPPENED BEFORE MY WORRY STARTED
HOW MY BODY FELT	STRATEGY I USED TO FEEL BETTER	NOTES

WORRY TRACKER

DATE :

MY WORRY	TIME & PLACE	WHAT HAPPENED BEFORE MY WORRY STARTED

HOW MY BODY FELT	STRATEGY I USED TO FEEL BETTER	NOTES

WORRY TRACKER

DATE :

| MY WORRY | TIME & PLACE | WHAT HAPPENED BEFORE MY WORRY STARTED |

| HOW MY BODY FELT | STRATEGY I USED TO FEEL BETTER | NOTES |

WORRY TRACKER

WORRY TRACKER

DATE :

MY WORRY	TIME & PLACE	WHAT HAPPENED BEFORE MY WORRY STARTED
HOW MY BODY FELT	STRATEGY I USED TO FEEL BETTER	NOTES

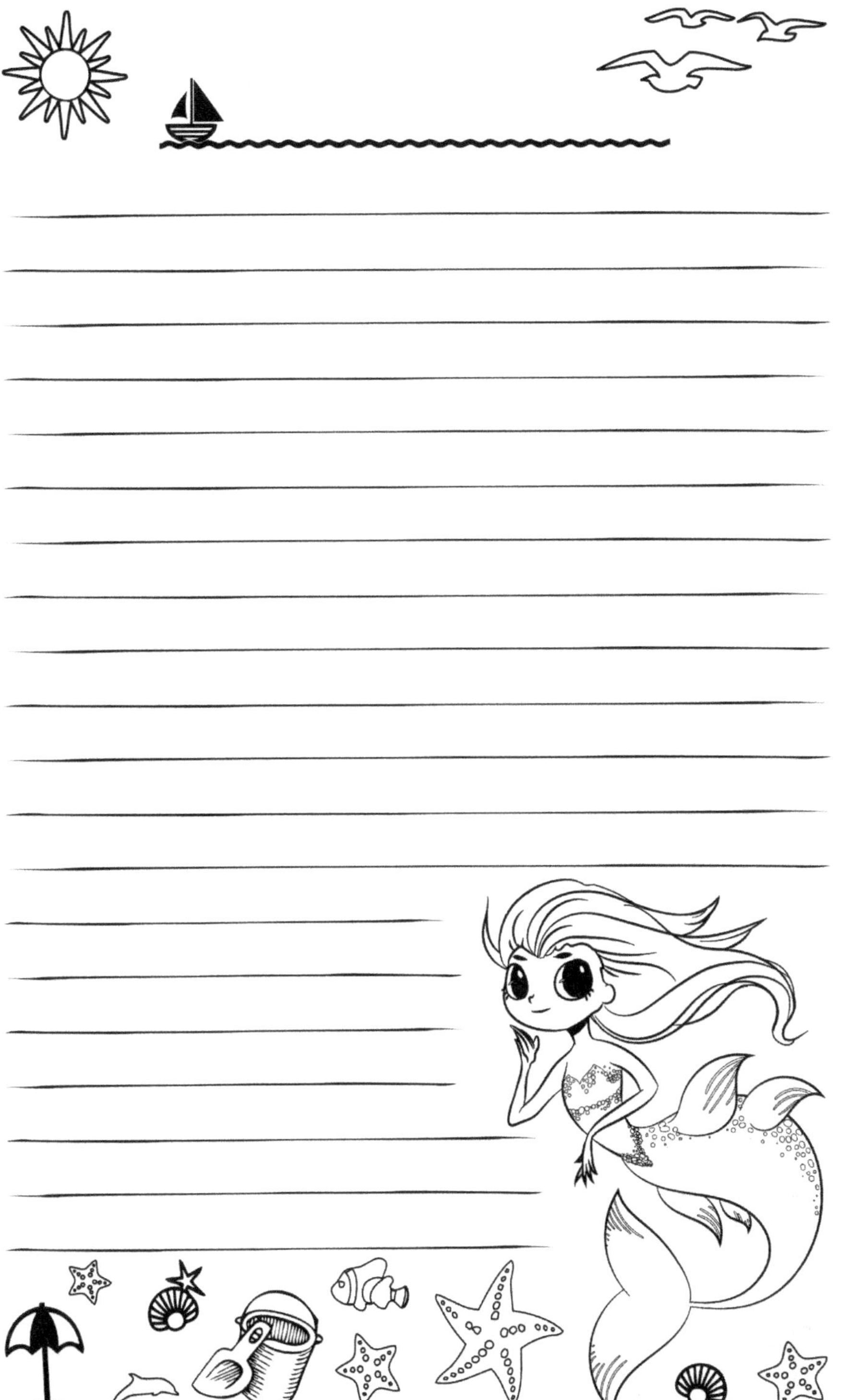